# Billy the K

## Story written by Gill Munton
## Illustrated by Tim Archbold

# Speed Sounds

**Consonants**   *Ask children to say the sounds.*

| f | l | m | n | r | s | v | z | **sh** | **th** | ng |
|---|---|---|---|---|---|---|---|---|---|---|
| ff | **ll** | | nn | | **ss** | ve | zz | | | nk |
| | | | | | | | s | | | |

| b | c | d | g | h | j | p | qu | t | w | x | y | ch |
|---|---|---|---|---|---|---|---|---|---|---|---|---|
| bb | k | | gg | | | pp | | tt | wh | | | tch |
| | ck | | | | | | | | | | | |

*Each box contains one sound but sometimes more than one grapheme.*
*Focus graphemes for this story are **circled**.*

## Vowels

*Ask children to say the sounds in and out of order.*

| a | e | i | o | u |
|---|---|---|---|---|
| at | hen | in | on | up |

| ay | ee | igh | ow | oo |
|----|----|-----|----|----|
| day | see | high | blow | zoo |

# Story Green Words

*Ask children to read the words first in Fred Talk and then say the word.*

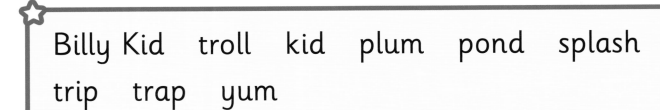

Billy  Kid   troll   kid   plum   pond   splash
trip   trap   yum

# Red Words

| | | |
|---|---|---|
| said | the | I |
| me | you | no |
| are | your | he |
| be | go | put |

# Billy the Kid

Billy the Kid, his mum and his dad

the big, bad troll

"Let me cross!" said Billy the Kid.
"Let me get a fat red plum."

"No," said the big bad troll.

"Let me cross!" said Mum.

"Let me get a fat red plum."

"No," said the troll.

"Let me cross!" said Dad.

"Let me get a fat red plum."

"No," said the troll.

Dad said, "Then I will put you in the pond!"

Splash!

"Help! Help!"

Trip trap
Trip trap
Trip trap

"Yum, yum!"

# Questions to talk about

*Ask children to TTYP for each question using 'Fastest finger' (FF) or 'Have a think' (HaT).*

**p.8**   (FF)    Who are the characters in the story?

**p.9**   (FF)    What did Billy say?

**p.10**  (FF)    What did the troll say?

**p.11**  (FF)    What did Dad say?

**p.12**  (FF)    What did Dad say? What did the troll say?

**p.13**  (HaT)  What made the trip trap noise?